BRIDGES
Engineering Masterpieces

*Ice bridge,
Los Glaciares
National Park,
Argentina*

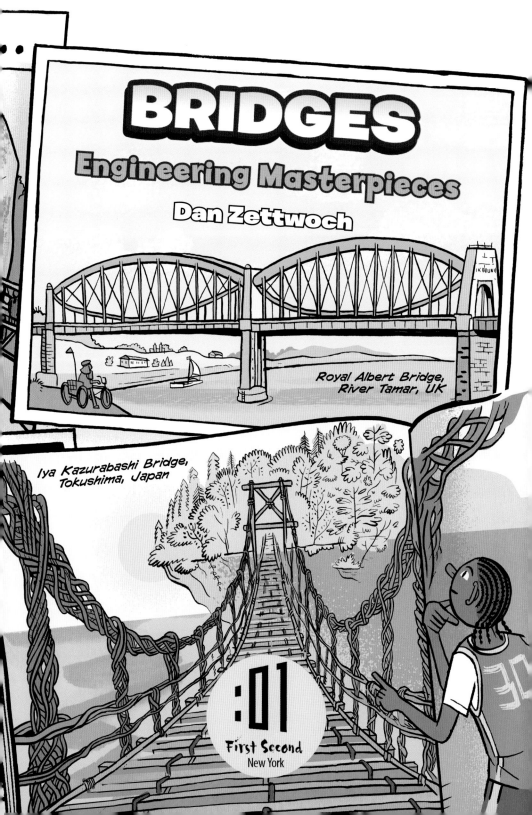

BRIDGES
Engineering Masterpieces
Dan Zettwoch

Royal Albert Bridge, River Tamar, UK

Iya Kazurabashi Bridge, Tokushima, Japan

:01

First Second
New York

First Second

Published by First Second
First Second is an imprint of Roaring Brook Press,
a division of Holtzbrinck Publishing Holdings Limited Partnership
120 Broadway, New York, NY 10271
firstsecondbooks.com
mackids.com

Library of Congress Cataloging-in-Publication Data is available.

Our books may be purchased in bulk for promotional, educational, or business use. Please
contact your local bookseller or the Macmillan Corporate and Premium Sales Department
at (800) 221-7945 ext. 5442 or by email at MacmillanSpecialMarkets@macmillan.com.

First edition, 2022
Edited by Dave Roman and Tim Stout
Cover design and interior book design by Dan Zettwoch and Sunny Lee
Bridge consultant: Stuart Nielsen

Penciled with Prismacolor Col-Erase non-repro blue pencil. Inked with Kuretake Pocket Brush Pen and Pentel Presto!
Jumbo White-out Pen. Colored with vectors in Adobe Illustrator along with my son Archie's cheap watercolor paints.

Printed in July 2022 in China by Toppan Leefung Printing Ltd., Dongguan City, Guangdong Province

ISBN 978-1-250-21690-8 (paperback)
10 9 8 7 6 5 4 3

ISBN 978-1-250-21689-2 (hardcover)
10 9 8 7 6 5 4 3 2

Don't miss your next favorite book from First Second! For the latest updates go
to firstsecondnewsletter.com and sign up for our enewsletter.

Stonecutters Bridge,
Rambler Channel,
Hong Kong

Have you ever wondered why bridges don't fall down? A big bridge weighs many thousands of tons, and yet it appears to hang effortlessly in the air across an estuary, a deep gorge, or whatever it is spanning. And then you go and whack a line of heavy trucks on it in each direction, and it still doesn't fall down—at least you hope it doesn't just as you begin to drive across it! Well, that's thanks to the clever engineers who have worked out how to make it stand up safely under all the various loads and extreme conditions it has to cope with.

But that's just the start of what engineers do. They must think about what materials to use, where those materials have to come from, and how long they will last. This is because we have to be careful not to use up the earth's limited resources, and we don't want to use materials that are harmful to the environment. And then there's the problem of how to build. Imagine trying to construct a long-span bridge out over the water— you can't exactly stand a crane out there, can you? So how can you lift the pieces into position?

Engineers use science to answer questions like, "How can I make this work?" or "What happens if I try this?" Science is cool, and without it, engineers could not do what they have to do. Using the results of scientific experiments combined with a practical understanding of physics, engineers are able to work out how to do amazing things! So, for example, a scientist might discover how to make a strong material like steel even stronger by adding extra elements or using different processes during its manufacture, and then engineers can work out practical methods for how and when to use the new, stronger material when it comes to their next project.

As someone who designs them for a living, I can tell you that every single bridge is different—because every bridge location is different! Before anyone starts building, several factors need to be considered. The engineer must decide what type of bridge is best depending on all sorts of factors, like how long it needs to be, whether it is in a city or the country, the nature of the landscape, how easy it is to build, budget concerns, and more. Also, the bridge must look good! At least, I think it should, because you wouldn't want a world full of ugly bridges, would you? I try to make my bridges beautiful so that they're not just useful but something aesthetically pleasing that people will actually appreciate, like they would a work of art! But what looks right in one place may not be the best idea in another. There's a lot to think about, and what I really love about bridge design is that it combines science with art and architecture to make things both functional and attractive.

I love the four main characters in this book. Bea, Archie, Trudy, and Spence each have a preference for a certain type of bridge, and they all get excited about how to use scientific facts and technical knowledge to come up with the best solution for each bridge. And the other thing is that they work as a team. They don't always agree (it would be very boring if they did!), but they work things out together. This is exactly how it works in reality, too. I always work in a team, and you never know where the best ideas will come from. Sometimes the best ideas can be really unexpected, and a brilliant new solution that you have never thought of before can emerge. It is a lot of fun!

So the next time you cross a bridge, you can ask yourself what materials have been used, which bits are carrying the loads, and how it all works together to make it safe for you to cross. And you can also ask yourself what you do or don't like about it or whether you think it looks good in the landscape. Has the engineer done a good job and successfully applied both the art and the science of engineering in the design? I hope you will be able to say yes to that question if you ever encounter one of my bridges!

—Ian Firth,
bridge designer

A daring circus owner.

A nervous steelworker.

An overconfident chief engineer.

Thousands of excited onlookers, eager to see the crossing.

4

Club motto: "WE HANG AROUND BRIDGES!"

The BATS mission: to visit and catalog the world's oldest, largest, most structurally innovative, and just plain battiest* bridges.

Pace yourself, young man!

We've got a long way to travel!

I got this! Y'all just tell me where to go!

*from "batty," /'badé/ adjective. Definition: crazy; insane. (Although, like bridges, we know bats to be brilliant and complex creatures.

BEFORE BRIDGES!

Goat Canyon, California, USA

Xiao River, Hebei Province, China

The Firth* of Forth, Scotland

*"Firth," an inlet of the sea

The Golden Gate, California, USA

Awesome, but missing something.

Like, what do you do if you need to get from here...

...to there?

11

I *observe* the other side of the bay and wanna get there. And I *don't* observe a jetpack or trampoline nearby.

Great, Bea! Let's move forward using the trusty ol' *scientific method.*

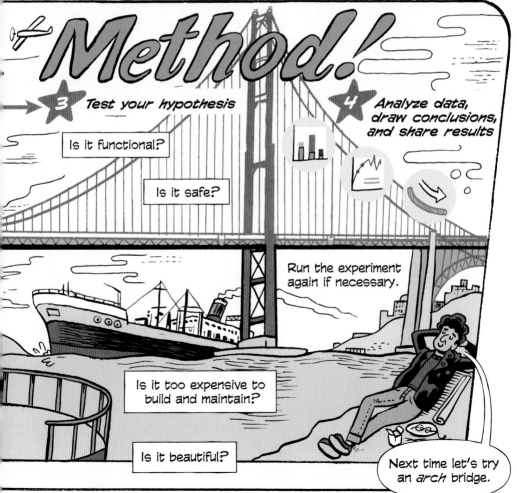

Method!

3 Test your hypothesis

Is it functional?

Is it safe?

4 Analyze data, draw conclusions, and share results

Run the experiment again if necessary.

Is it too expensive to build and maintain?

Is it beautiful?

Next time let's try an *arch* bridge.

So what is a *beam*, anyway?

As far as bridges go, it's *the simplest structural form*.

That's why I like it. Straight and to the point.

The word "beam" comes from Old English for "living tree."

Now a beam can be made of anything, like steel or concrete.

A beam can even be made of sunlight.

But I prefer the night.

Ooh, you're so mysterious, Bea.

You've heard of a balance beam.

My favorite is the laser beam.

But you can't walk on one of those. Yet.

The beam is probably the type of bridge you use the most. A common example is the basic highway overpass.

DECK

ABUTMENT

SPAN

PIER/ COLUMN

For definitions, see the glossary! pgs. 116-119

Follow me across the world's most interesting beams. Learn: A) what we use them for and B) how they're built to overcome any threats that come their way. Threats like these:

LOADS & FORCES

Try to keep up.

We'll keep up! Just like your hairdo!

Type: **Clapper bridge**
Material: **Stone slabs**
Total length: **55 m**
Longest span: ≈ **2.6 m**
Clearance: ≈ **1 m**
Opened: **Possibly Bronze Age, more likely c. 1400 CE**

This is a continuous beam with multiple spans—17 of them—supported by stone piers.

At two tons each, these dudes should be pretty sturdy.

But be careful, BATS. These stones get slippery with moss and water.

Not to mention the Devil's suntan lotion!

The BATS head far east to the mouth of the Luoyang River to cross one of the four ancient bridges of China:

LUOYANG BRIDGE 洛阳桥

EARLY SEA-CROSSING BEAM

Now this is a bridge to stroll on and feel perfectly safe.

An important link in the trading route known as the "Maritime Silk Road."

Bridge traffic: Pedestrian, livestock, carts, merchandise
Traffic beneath: Small boats

Agreed! And I'm glad to get to a bridge I can ride my trike across.

22

Let's take a break from the beam bridges and get heavy. Let's talk about *loads*.

A *load* is a weight or kind of pressure. There are three kinds of loads that affect bridges. The first type:

DEAD LOADS

This is the weight of the bridge itself. It's the stuff the bridge is made of: rock, wood, concrete, steel, cables, rivets, decorative stone lions, etc.

Some bridges are light and delicate. Others are massive and have a gigantic dead load, like the *Howrah Bridge* in West Bengal, India.

Then there are the temporary loads that move across the bridge: people, livestock, wagons full of goods, motor vehicles, etc. These are called:

LIVE LOADS

Because live loads are always changing, they are trickier to plan for.

The Howrah Bridge is super busy, carrying more than 100,000 vehicles and 150,000 pedestrians a day. That's a lotta live load.

Why aren't we visiting that one?

I don't like crowds.

There are other types of environmental loads—vandalism or sabotage, for instance—but a very dangerous one for metal bridges is *corrosion*.

Among iron and steel bridges, *rust* is a constant threat.

Even the chemicals in bird poop can cause metal to disintegrate.

On December 28, 1879, the Tay Bridge was up against all three types of loads. The bridge's deck of heavy iron girders (*dead load*) was being crossed by a rumbling locomotive (*live load*) during a violent storm (*environmental load*). The rest is history.

Hey, Bea. I guess loads weaken the structure of your hairdo, too, huh?

Now the BATS are in the middle of nowhere, peering over the edge of a steep valley. They're looking at a massive wooden framework known as the:

GOAT CANYON

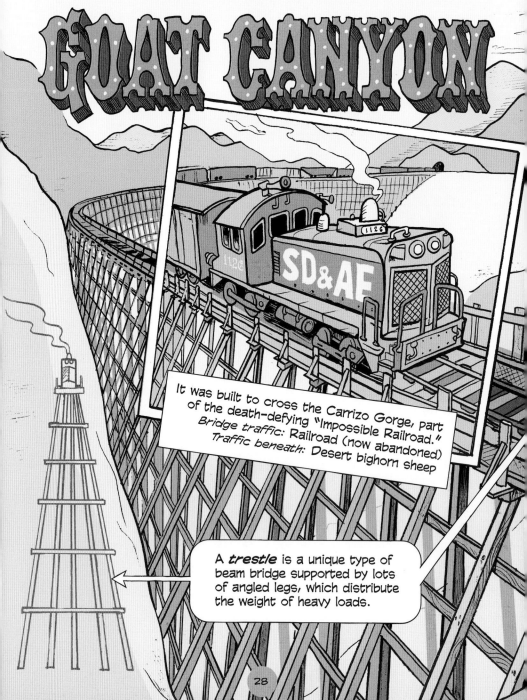

It was built to cross the Carrizo Gorge, part of the death-defying "Impossible Railroad."
Bridge traffic: Railroad (now abandoned)
Traffic beneath: Desert bighorn sheep

A *trestle* is a unique type of beam bridge supported by lots of angled legs, which distribute the weight of heavy loads.

28

Dudes. We know bridges handle *loads*. But how? Exactly what is happening when we drive a heavy station wagon across a bridge? Let's look at:

FORCES!

Like the forces of good and evil?

Kinda.

What is force?

In science, a *force* is any kind of pull or push on an object.

PULL

PUSH

A force can cause an object to move or to stop.

PFF

The object can remain in place if the forces are balanced.

The object can be *deformed* and change shape.

Uh, Archie. You might not wanna be deforming Grandma's fuzzy dice.

Force is measured in **newtons** (N), thanks to Sir Isaac Newton.

While studying objects, forces, and motion, he defined the laws of the natural phenomenon known as:

GRAVITY!

His law of universal gravitation says that bigger objects attract smaller objects toward them.

MOON mass: m

EARTH mass: M

Gravity is not technically a force. The theory of relativity redefines it to be an effect of the curvature in the fabric of space-time.

Thanks, Einstein!

Either way, gravity is always trying to pull things down.

So for bridges, the effect of gravity is the major force to be reckoned with.

⸮Gulp⸮

COMPRESSION

Grab the AFM.* With this dude, we can take a super-close look.

*Atomic force microscope

ATOM

WOOD MOLECULE

CHEMICAL BOND

Now when I press down on the beam you can see...

...how the wood fibers inside are being *squished together*.

This is the force of *compression*.

When I remove the load, the force is released.

The molecules spring back.

SPROING!

We call that *elasticity*.

KOCHER VIADUCT

aka Kochertalbrücke

Type: **Box girder beam**
Material: **Prestressed concrete**
Total length: **1,128 m**
Longest span: **138 m**
Max clearance: **185 m**
Opened: **1979**

I'm not afraid of bridges. ≥Gulp≤ I love bridges.

It's okay, Spence! It's good to respect the forces of nature. We *are* soaring through the sky on a few bits of concrete.

Okay then. I'm terrified.

The bending forces in the middle of each span are the same as the ruler: the top surface gets slightly shorter (squished by *compression*), the bottom gets slightly longer (stretched apart in *tension*).

That's why the beam is shaped like an empty box: more material at the top and bottom is stronger. That's also why many beams are shaped like an "I."

If you wanted to remember those four types of forces—our rivals!—just remember what they start with:

Compression
(squishing)

and

Tension
(stretching)

Torsion
(twisting)

Shear
(sliding)

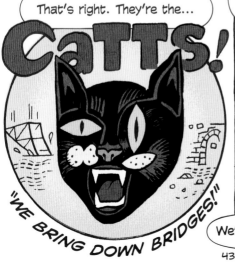

That's right. They're the...

CaTTS!

"WE BRING DOWN BRIDGES!"

C'mon, really?! A cutesy critter acronym?!

That's beneath us.

We're the BATS. Everything is beneath us.

43

Structural engineers use a kind of "X-ray vision" to see how forces impact the bones of built structures.

Luckily for us, bridges have fully visible skeletons. We don't have to peel away layers of walls and stuff to see how they work. But it does take training to "see" the invisible CaTTS at work.

What do you mean "invisible"? I see them all! Aw...kitties.

Just kidding.

WINK!

Okay...my turn!

Let's look at the *best* kind of bridges...

Check out the long-lasting power of these ARCHES!

Type: **Multi-arch aqueduct**
Material: **Granite blocks**
Aboveground length: **728 m**
Longest span: **5 m**
Height: **28.5 m**
Opened: **c. 112 CE**

180°

Romans used lots of semicircular arches in sequence, which distribute the compression forces nicely. *Arches experience primarily compression.*

Stone is very strong when it comes to compression, so it works great for arches.

Usually we think of bridges carrying people over water, not vice versa.

I guess *agua* was as important back then as it is now.

BATS reusable water bottles available now!

Rather than a semicircular arch, the Anji Bridge uses a smaller segment of a circle for its curve.

Type: **Segmental arch bridge**
Material: **Limestone slabs**
Opened: **605 CE (Sui Dynasty)**
Total length: **50.8 m**
Longest span: **37.4 m**
Height: **7.23 m**

90°

It also introduces these clever arched openings called spandrels, which allow high waters through.

They also allow the bridge to use less material and feel more graceful.

"It's a crescent moon rising from the clouds."

How poetic. Did you make that up yourself?

I read it on the plaque next to the bridge.

After steel, the next major revolution in materials came with *concrete*. Basic concrete has been around since ancient times. This Mesopotamian bridge was built in 690 BCE using waterproof cement.

The Jerwan Aqueduct, Iraq

CONCRETE

needs three ingredients mixed together: *Water*

Aggregate, which can be sand, gravel, crushed stone, etc.

Cement, which is usually a powder made from limestone.

Pour your concrete into the shape you need and let it harden.

BLOCK

FLAT

BATS

DECORATIVE/OTHER

Concrete is everywhere. We've covered the world with it.

But we didn't know its true strength until this little trick...

REINFORCED CONCRETE

Pouring concrete around steel reinforcing bars (aka *rebar*) creates a material that handles loads and forces with the best of both worlds.

Concrete: strong in compression but weak in tension, cracking easily

Steel: strong in tension, helping concrete not to crack

The cave-like *Alvord Lake Bridge* in San Francisco, California, is America's oldest reinforced concrete bridge.

Now this is a good place for BATS to hang out!

65

66

SECTION ③ TRUSS BRIDGES

Try angles!

ALSO!

Design! How are bridges shaped?

Bonus! Build DIY model bridges...

...for fun and profit!

Trudy, what's with you and triangles?

Triangles are just terrific! They're the strongest geometric shape. Look at these toothpick structures:

Look how easily you can shear and deform the square.

You can't do that to a triangle.

The word "truss" comes from Old French for "a collection of things bundled together."

Truss structures were first used as roof supports.

KING POST ROOF TRUSS

Early timber truss bridges could be found in heavily forested countries like Switzerland.

Now there's an "Integrated Truss Structure" on the International Space Station.

PONY TRUSS

DECK TRUSS

The previous trusses are considered "through trusses" (because you pass through them). A "pony truss" is only half-height.

Deck trusses look like they've been built upside down!

FINK TRUSS

WICHERT TRUSS

These were all attempts to maximize the strength of a bridge while minimizing the cost. Builders didn't want to spend so much money on wood, iron, or steel.

However, the builders of this next bridge spared no expense.

MULTI-SPAN CANTILEVER THROUGH TRUSS

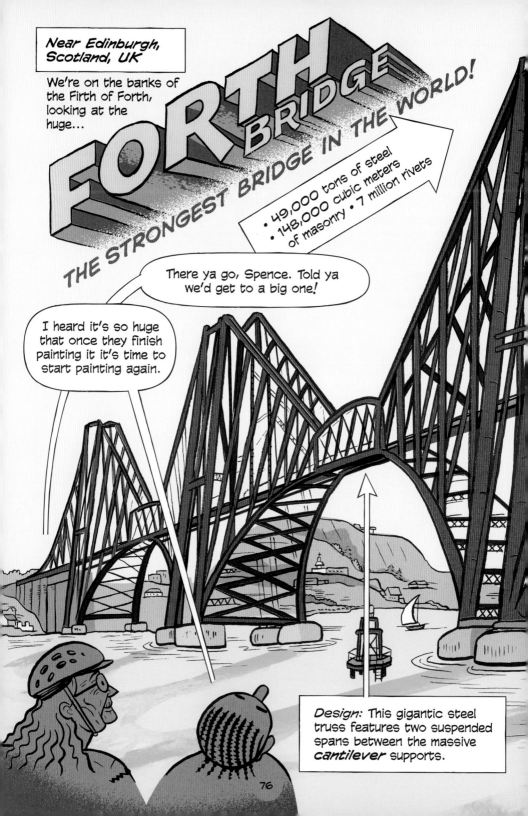

Near Edinburgh, Scotland, UK

We're on the banks of the Firth of Forth, looking at the huge...

FORTH BRIDGE

THE STRONGEST BRIDGE IN THE WORLD!

- 49,000 tons of steel
- 148,000 cubic meters of masonry • 7 million rivets

There ya go, Spence. Told ya we'd get to a big one!

I heard it's so huge that once they finish painting it it's time to start painting again.

Design: This gigantic steel truss features two suspended spans between the massive *cantilever* supports.

Type: **Cantilever truss**
Material: **Steel**
Total length: **2,467 m**
Spans: ≈ **518 m**
Height: **110 m**
Max clearance: **46 m**
Opened: **1890**

CANTILEVER   CANTILEVER
SUSPENDED
SPAN

Y'all got me?

Here are the BATS demonstrating the *cantilever* principle with young
Spence suspended between horizontal supports. Try this at home!

79

Puente de la Mujer,
Buenos Aires, Argentina

SWING BRIDGE

Vizcaya Bridge, Biscay, Spain

TRANSPORTER BRIDGE

Okay...

This is officially the weirdest bridge so far.

Ganges River Bridge,
Allahabad, India

PONTOON BRIDGE

SECTION 4

It's hang time!

SUSPENSION

ALSO!

BRIDGES

Construction!
How are bridges built?

Bonus!
Cable-stayed bridges...

...and more!

Y'all know that *suspension* bridges have been around for a while, right?

Spiders have been building 'em for millions of years.

These webs are all tension and are really strong for how light they are.

From the Latin for "hang under," that's exactly what suspension bridges do.

They're sort of like arches, just upside down.

We often say bridges are "living things" but it's really true of India's

living root bridges.

This is taken to a new level by army ants who build suspension bridges out of...themselves!

Ew!

Look in my sketchbook. This shows the parts of a suspension bridge. Lemme draw in how they balance *compression* and *tension*.

Scientists study the natural world through experiments and observations.

Engineers apply that knowledge and create the BUILT environment.

ENGINEERS!

CIVIL ENGINEERS
This broad category, distinguished from military engineers, goes way back.

We're in charge of large projects like:

AIRPORTS

ROADS

RAIL TRANSPORT

WATER SYSTEMS AND SEWERS

ETC.

STRUCTURAL ENGINEERS
This subcategory of builders specializes in load-bearing structures.

We focus on building and maintaining:

BUILDINGS

ROLLER COASTERS

BRIDGES

DAMS

ETC.

Thangtong Gyalpo was also a Buddhist master, yogi, doctor, architect, and theater troupe leader!

Hey, I sing a little bit here and there!

One of the earliest civil engineers to become a household name was Thomas Telford, aka "The Colossus of Roads."

Menai Suspension Bridge, Anglesey, North Wales

A well-known modern bridge builder is Santiago Calatrava, whose works are stylish, sculptural, and often controversial.

Doesn't really fit in...

The Bridge of Strings, Jerusalem, Israel

The Iraqi-British architect Zaha Mohammad Hadid has made many swirling, geometrically challenging bridges, giving her the nickname "The Queen of Curves."

Now that's more like it!

Sheikh Zayed Bridge, Abu Dhabi, UAE

This beautiful bridge is the result of one famous bridge-building family.

BROOKLYN BRIDGE

The ROEBLINGS

After her father-in-law John's death and husband Washington's illness, Emily oversaw completion of this landmark.

JOHN   WASHINGTON   EMILY

Construction method: The towers are sunk deep into the river and rest on giant underwater *caissons*. Workers (and Washington himself) got sick working in these pressurized boxes with a new disease called "the bends."

I mentioned them earlier, but let's take a closer look at a few

CABLE-STAYED BRIDGES!

They look similar to suspension bridges but are actually quite different.

Cable-stayed bridges don't have large, curved suspension cables joining the towers with smaller cables hanging down. They have straight cables directly connecting the bridge deck to the towers.

Cavenagh Bridge, Singapore

The cables have a triangular, fanlike design or a series of parallel diagonal lines.

Most SNP, aka UFO Bridge, Bratislava, Slovakia

Guizhou and Yunnan Provinces, China

The BATS reach the last bridge in this year's expedition, an intimidating cable-stayed beast.

It's like the final boss.

Construction method: China has been going through a bridge-building explosion. Most of the world's highest bridges call this mountainous region home. Extreme geological conditions force bridges higher and higher.

110

111

BASIC BRIDGE

Sydney Harbor Bridge, New South Wales, Australia

ABUTMENT

ARCH TRUSS

SUSPENDER HANGERS

DECK

CENTRAL

FOUNDATION

LOADS

DEAD LOAD

LIVE LOAD

ENVIRONMENTAL LOAD

PARTS

TOP CHORD

DIAGONAL

APPROACH SPAN

BOTTOM CHORD

SPAN

BATS MARKER COMPRESSION!

BATS MARKER TENSION!

WATERPROOF

NON-TOXIC

FORGES

NOT PICTURED:

Torsion (twisting)

Shear (sliding)

Compression (squishing)

Tension (stretching)

GLOSSARY

Abutment a structure supporting the end of a bridge, especially an arch

Aggregate the sand, gravel, or stone mixed with cement to form concrete

Aqueduct a bridge that carries water

Arch a curved structure spanning an opening, mostly under compression

Bascule a movable bridge that rotates from a horizontal to a vertical position; French for "see-saw"

Beam a straight structure spanning one support to another, experiencing compression and tension

Bioengineering the use of biological organisms or processes in design or construction

Blast furnace an industrial tower that uses hot compressed air to turn iron ore into usable metals

Box girder a hollow structural beam, typically with a square, rectangular, or trapezoidal cross-section

Breaking point the moment of greatest strain before a material fractures

Cable a collection of strands or a bundle of parallel wires forming a thick rope

Cable-stayed bridge a bridge in which the deck is directly supported by cables attached to towers, usually in a fanlike or diagonal pattern

Caisson a watertight chamber used while constructing bridge foundations in water

Cantilever a structure that extends freely beyond its supporting pier

Cast iron iron/carbon alloy that is hard, brittle, and strong in compression

Causeway a long, raised road over low or wet ground

Cement a powder that mixes with water and aggregate to form concrete

Chord the outer parts of a truss structure that defines its shape

Clapper bridge an ancient type of beam bridge made from piles of stones

Compression a "squishing" force that pushes a material together and makes it shorter

Concrete a mixture of aggregate, water, and cement that hardens into a stonelike material

Corbeled arch an opening formed by stacks of blocks gradually pushing inward

Covered bridge a bridge protected from environmental loads with a roof

Dead load the weight of the bridge material itself

Deck the surface part of a bridge that is a road, rail, or walkway

Deform to change the physical shape of a material through force

Drawbridge *see* movable bridge

Elasticity the ability of a material to spring back to its original shape after a deforming force is released

Engineer a person who designs, builds, and maintains structures, machines, or public works

Environmental load a dynamic load, often weather-related

Factor of safety a margin built into the hypothesized strength of a structure

Force an influence that pulls, pushes, or changes direction of an object

Foundation the lowest load-supporting part of a bridge

Gephyrophobia the fear of bridges

Gravity the natural phenomenon that pulls structures toward the earth

Hypothesis a proposed explanation that must be tested

I-beam a structural member with an I-shaped cross-section

Iron ore a raw metallic element used in cast or wrought iron and steel

Keystone the wedge-like piece placed in the center of an arch

Live load a dynamic load such as vehicular or pedestrian traffic

Load the weight carried by a structure

Masonry stone, brick, or concrete block construction

Materials the physical matter from which a bridge is made

Mortar a paste of cement, sand, and water used in masonry

Movable bridge a bridge with moving parts that can transform to allow through passage

Natural bridge a rock formation where an arch has formed

Pedestrian bridge a bridge used by walkers and often cyclists

Pier a column that supports the spans of a bridge

Pontoon bridge a bridge that floats on the water's surface

Pony truss a short through truss with an open top

Prestressing applying forces to a material to deform it, making it stronger during use

Reinforced concrete concrete with steel bars inside to increase strength and durability

Rust a type of corrosion that's damaging to iron and steel

Segmental arch a curved segment of an arch that's less than a semicircle

Shear a "sliding" force parallel to the surface of a material

Slide rule a mechanical engineer's tool before calculators or computers

Span the distance between bridge supports

Steel strong, durable iron/carbon alloy

Strain how far a material is deformed due to stress

Strand many wires twisted together

Strength the amount of stress needed to break a material

Stress the amount of force pushing or pulling on an area of material

Substructure the lower part of a bridge (i.e., abutments and piers) that supports the superstructure

Superstructure the upper part of a bridge (i.e., deck and towers) that carries traffic

Suspender hanger a vertical cable, rod, or bar connecting the main cable of a suspension bridge to the deck

Suspension bridge a bridge in which the deck is supported by hangers attached to a main cable strung between towers

Tension a "stretching" force that pulls a material apart and makes it longer

Torsion a "twisting" force

THE ECHOLOCATOR
1960 Dodge six-passenger station wagon with 318 V8

ATOMIC FORCE MICROSCOPE

SPAGHETTI ARCH BRIDGE (UNDESTROYED)

ROAD–RAIL WHEEL ATTACHMENTS

NOVELTY T-SHIRT FROM BLOUKRANS BRIDGE BUNGEE JUMP

Tower a tall structure supporting the main cables of a suspension bridge or cable-stayed bridge

Trestle a framework bridge built on many pairs of angled legs

True arch *see* arch

Truss a structure of many parts arranged and connected together, usually in triangles

Viaduct a bridge made from many small spans

Voussoired arch an opening formed by a smooth curve of wedge-shaped blocks

Wrought iron iron alloy that contains little carbon and is softer than cast iron or steel

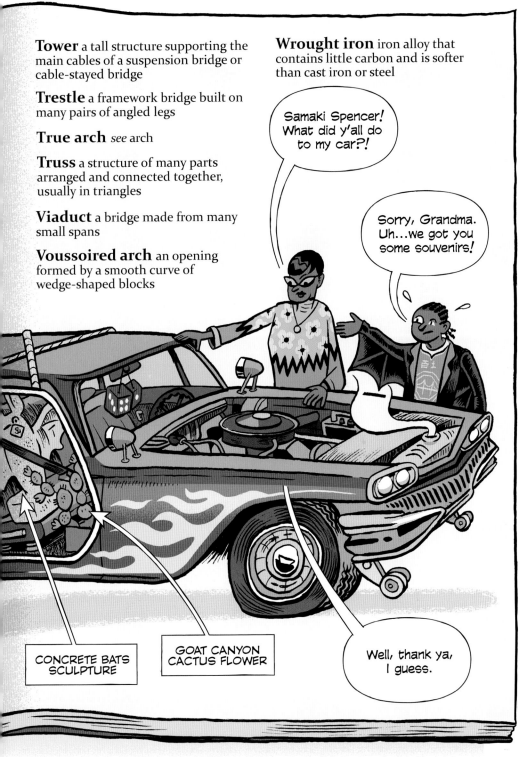

BiBLiOGRAPHY

Agrawal, Roma. *Built: The Hidden Stories Behind Our Structures.* Bloomsbury USA, 2018.

Blockley, David. *Bridges: The Science and Art of the World's Most Inspiring Structures.* Oxford University Press, 2012.

Dupré, Judith. *Bridges: A History of the World's Most Spectacular Spans.* Black Dog & Leventhal, 2017.

Gordon, J.E. *Structures: Or Why Things Don't Fall Down.* Da Capo Press, 2003.

Isaac, P.M. *A Critical Analysis of the Bloukrans Bridge.* University of Bath, 2007.

Karas, Slawomir and Nien-Tsu Tuan. "The World's Oldest Bridges - Mycenaean Bridges." *American Journal of Civil Engineering and Architecture,* 2017, Vol. 5, No. 6, 237–244.

Loomis, Richard Thomas. *The History of the Building of the Golden Gate Bridge.* Stanford University, 1958.

Mars, Roman and Emmett FitzGerald. "Rebar and the Alvord Lake Bridge" and "The Batman and the Bridge Builder." 99% Invisible. Podcast audio episodes #81 and #432, 2013 and 2021.

McCullough, David. *The Great Bridge: The Epic Story of the Building of the Brooklyn Bridge.* Simon & Schuster, 1983.

Miller, Howard and Quinta Scott. *The Eads Bridge.* Missouri History Museum Press, 1999.

Petroski, Henry. *To Engineer Is Human: The Role of Failure in Successful Design.* Vintage, 1992.

Sevaistre, Bruno. *The Bridge in the Sky: Millau Viaduct* (documentary). MagellanTV, 2016.

The St. Louis Republican. "The Bridge: The Elephant Declares It a Good Piece of Work—An Immense Crowd of Sight-Seers Yesterday." Monday Morning, June 15, 1874.

Zhia Dao, *History of Transportation in China* (eBook). Kobo, 2019.

These websites were helpful in double-checking bridge specifications:
bridgehunter.com
highestbridges.com
structurae.net

Acknowledgments! The first bridge I remember crossing was the Sherman Minton Bridge (double-decker through arch) connecting the West End of Louisville, Kentucky, to New Albany, Indiana. Love you, Mom and Dad!

Dedication! This book is for Leslie and (our son) Archie, who I hope continues to cross all kinds of bridges, try different things, and make new connections over the span of his entire life.